Dirty Talk

Dirty Talking Tips That Will Make Your Partner Go Crazy
and Help You Have the Time of Your Life

*(In a Flash Get Her Wet With These Scandalous Sexts and
Dirty Words)*

Duane Lagace

TABLE OF CONTENT

The Influence Of Exuding Self-Assurance 1

Throwing Seeds For The Future Date 12

Ways To Make Your Physical Appearance Better .. 34

Add Your Own Principles And Beliefs. 51

Have A Deep Conversation With Your Significant Other. 83

What Are The Advantages Of Tantric Practice? ... 109

Typical Blunders Males Make When Speaking With Women 134

The Influence Of Exuding Self-Assurance

Hello, lovely! Do you want to know how to draw in the right kind of men and turn off the wrong ones? It's easy: exude confidence like a pro! When a woman exudes unwavering confidence and self-assurance, men find it impossible to resist them. Prepare to embrace your inner queen and learn the impact of projecting confidence!

Being confident attracts others to you in the same way as a magnet does. A confident demeanor conveys a strong message that you value and believe in yourself.

Enjoy Some Self-Care

Allow me to reveal the secret: self-care is your neglected component! It's not about trying to fit into unrealistic ideals or spending hours in front of the mirror.

Now, let's dispel a few myths. It's not about wearing excessive makeup or being the skinniest person in the room. No, no, no! Rather, it's all about accepting a holistic approach to self-care and accepting the skin you're in.

Prioritize taking care of your beautiful skin. Discover a skincare regimen that gives you a glamorous feeling. Give your skin the attention and affection it needs with a facial massage, a luxury moisturizer, or a hydrating face mask. Ultimately, glowing skin is the best way to increase self-assurance!

Let us move on to discussing your amazing mane. Accept the beauty that nature has given to your hair and establish a hair care regimen that makes you feel like a princess. Whether you have beautiful straight hair, delicious curls, or everything in between, never forget that your hair is an extension of your brilliant personality, and that confidence comes from the inside out.

Let's now go into the realm of body love! It's time to accept the skin you're in and enjoy your special curves. Recall that the goal is not to fit into a particular size or body type. It's about appreciating and respecting your body for everything it provides for you.

Engage in pursuits that give you a sense of strength, vitality, and aliveness. Find methods to move your body that make you happy and feel like the queen you are, whether it's yoga, dancing to your favorite music, or taking a cool swim.

Oh, and let's not overlook fashion, my dear! Wear something that reflects your style and gives you a royal feeling. Wear clothing that gives you a sense of self-assurance and ease, regardless of whether you choose to go with basic neutrals, bright hues, or vivid prints. Never forget that you are the masterpiece of fashion.

Finally, self-care is more than just looking good. It's about taking care of your spirit and intellect as well. Make time for the pursuits that offer you calm and serenity. Make your mental health a priority by reading a good book, practicing meditation, or keeping a record of your thoughts. Your confidence will shine through when your inner world is taken care of.

Moving On From the Past

As an undergraduate, I learned how to navigate the complex world of relationships and the value of moving on from the past as a woman. I met someone over summer vacation who won my heart and ignited a bond that felt so promising.

As our relationship grew, I couldn't help but see the residual effects of our previous disappointments and heartbreaks. It became clear that facing and letting go of the ghosts of our pasts was necessary to cultivate a happy and healthy union.

We set out on a voyage of introspection and candid dialogue together. We opened up about our anxieties, insecurities, and emotional baggage from past relationships. Although it was a delicate process, it set the stage for recovery and development.

With every meaningful discussion, we consciously choose to move past the past. We realized that holding on to the hurts of the past would only sour our relationship today and make it more difficult for us to build a future together. We were resolved to release ourselves from the bonds holding us back, even if it was a stark reality calling for grit and resiliency.

Our partnership was engulfed by a fresh sense of freedom and lightness as we released the burdens of the past. We accepted forgiveness—from those who had wronged us in the past and from ourselves. We cherished the love and happiness that grew between us and kept our attention on the here and now.

We could completely appreciate the beauty of our love by letting go of the past. We fostered trust, increased our emotional closeness, and established an environment conducive to authenticity and vulnerability. Without the gloom of the past obscuring our view, we supported one other's aspirations and rejoiced in each other's successes.

This event taught me that a woman must face and let go of her past to have a lively and satisfying relationship. Leaving behind the past allows love to grow in its purest form and creates new opportunities. Although it requires guts, integrity, and a readiness to accept vulnerability, the benefits are tremendous.

We all, darling, have a past that has shaped who we are today—fabulous people. Here's the kicker: there's a reason why the past doesn't go away. No man wants to listen to you bawl nonstop about your controlling parents, emotional rollercoaster relationships, and ex-lover. I promise you that a man can only take so much mental abuse.

Therefore, the key to attracting guys is to be respectful and considerate enough to accept your history without bringing it up in every interaction with your current partner.

Here's the thing: attracting a decent guy depends greatly on how you talk about your previous relationships. You're setting yourself up for a relationship full of misery if you can't stop talking about your ex or your previous dating mishaps. A lady who acknowledges her past without dwelling on her faults, disappointments, and bad experiences with her ex-partners will always captivate men. Taking responsibility for your history without allowing it to dictate your present or future is key.

Women who live in the past frequently compare and look for parallels in their current relationships with those from the past. Here's a tip: forget about the past and concentrate on the present. Just as much as we hate being compared to our ex-partners, men also detest being compared to them.

It's time to embrace the present and move on from the past, darling. Let go of the past and be present in your encounters. Demonstrate to your potential partner that you're prepared for a new beginning free from the burdens of the past. Let go of the past to make room for a happier and healthier relationship and to open yourself up to new possibilities.

Recall that the past is behind you for a purpose, my love. Thus, let's focus on the here and now, savor the present, and build a joyful, loving, and prosperous future. Irresistible charm and a positive outlook will attract the right man and leave the drama of the past behind. You should have a brand-new love tale free of the lingering effects of the past.

Throwing Seeds For The Future Date

It's hard to even get the correct words out of your mouth when the moment of fate draws near, especially if you genuinely like her. Tension and awkwardness rise.

This results from a fear of being rejected, not being accepted, and not appreciating it.

You should understand that a woman's "NO" does not always indicate that she dislikes you or is rejecting you. It indicates that you have approached her incorrectly or made an offer that she would find awkward to accept.

Furthermore, you must develop the ability to discern between a genuine

"NO" and a fake one. Many women will act as though you're refusing at first so as not to come out as pushy ladies. They want to observe how you handle things, whether you'll follow through, and whether you're serious about going out with them.

I'll show you how to overcome these obstacles and get you to say "yes" immediately!

Ascertaining that the date has already been arranged between you is the simplest approach to setting one up with a woman. If you follow this procedure, the time you officially request something—over the phone or in person—will be a formality!

We discussed how choosing an excellent restaurant for a traditional dinner outing on a first date can be inconvenient.

It makes no difference if she is a female you recently met, a friend, a colleague, or an acquaintance—what matters is that you can discuss with her.

It's not the best to talk about this and that and then ask her out of the blue. Similarly, it is not advised to obtain your number from untrusted sources or look up his profile on social media in a stalker-like manner. Remember that women are drawn to guys who are confident in their desires and do not hesitate to pursue them.

You need to ensure she's anxiously awaiting when you allow her to trade contact information. Since she is drawn to you, aware of her interest, and wants to see you again, she must want to offer you her number.

Let's examine how. Let's go back to our initial encounter with her.

In this initial talk, you will already have to assume certain possibilities of going on a date naturally without needing to know her response. You'll need to try to pique her interest by discussing your activities, programs, and daily routine.

As previously mentioned, the goal of the date is to get to know each other better. She needs to know who you are. Therefore, you can meet this need by introducing yourself to her before you date.

There is no magic word that may convince a woman to say yes because every person is unique and has their personality and desires. In any case, I've provided a few examples to assist you better grasp the idea.

Examples according to your potential areas of interest:

- "... you know, the first time I saw a capoeira performance, I was in Portugal when I returned; I enrolled in a course, you know it's fun; I see you well, you should come to try one day ..."
- "They recommended me a new clothing store in the centre, next week I will go for a jump as soon there will be the wedding of ..."
- "Almost every Sunday we go to this beach, by a friend

of mine, in few know it, it's a heavenly place, there is a lot of space and you can do what you want..." ● I've already been there just for the aperitif, which is amazing, and because of it, I've learned that jazz isn't all that horrible.

● "I would see you well subnet in volleyball, we play for fun in mixed teams a couple of times a month" ● "Yesterday at the salsa course we learned a spectacular figure, you should come and try you to a day of these..."

The idea of working with you on a project solidifies at this stage. You can be more precise by telling her that you will send her a message with the new dates and times if she says she's okay with the idea, such as, "Yes, how nice I would like to try." This will provide you with an excellent cause to gain her phone number.

I want to remind you that this initial discussion you have with her is helpful for sowing seeds you will soon reap. However, it is not required to set up a date.

This "planting" ensures that she will not forget you. She will recognize you when you call and want to talk to you. Most men—including myself—have encountered scenarios in which she either didn't answer the phone or, if she did, it took time to get her to recall who she was speaking to.

This occurs because the initial spark of attraction that you both felt evaporates a few minutes after you part ways, and it will be challenging to arouse her interest in going out with you or even just having a phone conversation if you don't leave her with anything to remember.

In addition to discussing your interests and pursuits, we see another tactic to establish a "docking point."

Keep her name in mind and give it to her a few times while you speak. Our name holds the utmost significance for every individual as it is a spoken directive that we are habituated to comply with from birth. She will attempt to remember your name after realizing you can recall hers. This will give her a favorable impression of you.

Establish collaboration to build a special connection between you. The simplest method to incite cooperation is to give it a creative, humorous moniker that makes her feel like a tomboy or a youngster. Nothing too suggestive, overly loving, or disrespectful; it needs to be something special that she will only identify with you. You'll have to devise a nickname for her that captures her unique personality, appearance, words, and mannerisms.

For instance, you may respond, "Ha-ha, then from now on, I'll call you "Miss Pocket Coffee," when she begins to gripe about her job and mentions that at this time, she consumes five coffees a day!

Since it's getting a little long, I'll just nickname you Pocket.

Use your imagination, but keep it contextual. No cutesy nicknames like Sister, Beauty, or Princess, etc. Cartoon character references are preferable.

Just calling her by that nickname in the future will bring back memories of the two of you and the attraction that existed at the moment.

Additionally, if she's clever and playful, she'll give you a nickname, which will help you both by giving you a special recollection of the two of you.

Other strategies for inciting complicity include:

Discussing more private and intimate subjects.

Cracking a little joke to a third party in attendance.

Revealing yourself to her or revealing a secret.

Hinting at a hypothetical future together (e.g., "you and I will end up meeting again in Hawaii").

Try to evoke strong feelings when you speak to her since the more time she spends thinking about you and the more she longs to meet you, the more memories she will have connected to you. Throughout the chat, be upbeat and energetic and speak kindly and passionately.

Chapter 3: A Five-Step Guide for Appropriate Use of Dirty Talk

Dirty conversation is one of the tastiest and simplest methods to liven up your romantic life and make sex something entirely different.

Many females enjoy testing out their dirty language in the bedroom, but the main barrier they face is usually fear:

The fear of not knowing how to respond.

The fear of embarrassing themselves and getting negative reactions.

The biggest concern is not knowing what to say. Here's

A 5-step strategy to help you avoid awkward situations and make the most of the time spent with your family.

Step 1: Start with a story-based type of trolling

Storytelling is the simplest way to engage in dirty conversation, especially when you are at a loss for words. A tale of dirt speech can be used for one of the five items:

a) What you intend to do; b) What is happening to you; c) What you are doing; d) How you feel; and e) What you wish to accomplish with yourself

Step 2: Hot Responses

Even before you engage in actual sex, you can start practicing seductive reactions, such as when you chat, flirt, or converse in public. You can speak out if your spouse asks, "Do you like that?" rather than just saying, "Yeah! It's heaven in me." It is crucial to remember that your responses must be concise, truthful, and helpful.

Step 3: Important queries

If your friend is more laid back than you are, try introducing some lighthearted questions to spice up your sex. Your inquiries are helpful, and responding to them shouldn't be too challenging. Some instances of flirtatious questions are:

"Are you going to like this child?"

Is that what you'd prefer?

And, my love, are I correct?

Step 4: Experiment with various words and noises

Your practice and inexperience play a major role in what makes dirty talking unique. It's also wise because you won't have to take a chance on what he saw in adult movies. Sighs, rumblings, groans, labored breathing, and speech should all sound brand-new.

Step 5: Examine your partner

With time, you can tell which phrases or words make him uncomfortable and which ones work for you. Do everything that drives him wild, even the sounds and words you utter. You should be aware that having sex is no longer a boring routine but rather a passionate experience that gets better as you pick up new words and behaviors.

Every woman would acknowledge that having sex is one crucial aspect of a relationship that cannot be sacrificed. As long as their sexual lives are respectable, every guy will also confess that they are willing to go to great lengths to make sure their marriage or partnership lasts forever.

Eliminating the monotony that permeates most marriages and intimate relationships is the largest difficulty, though. There is a pretty easy solution: engage in filthy conversation during sex. Even though it's fairly common, not all girls know how to use foul words properly. If it becomes embarrassing or humiliating, some people fire it once or twice and give up completely.

I'll give you some tips on what constitutes appropriate and inappropriate nasty conversation. Identifying the appropriate sources is the first piece of advice I can provide.

Don't just listen to your girlfriends and take their advice at face value.

Experts in these fields, sexologists, and sex therapists have produced several great eBooks and guides. You should take a look at one. Comprehending the true nature of dirty language and adhering to certain protocols are crucial to mastering its art.

Because males are different from women, you will learn what your partner enjoys and finds objectionable. You can start with basic phrases and charming texts if you're a shy girl. While your partner is away, you can create a romantic mood by flirting and sending him sultry texts on his phone.

If all goes well, it will help you gain confidence, establish communication, and provide the ground for healthy sex. This is where you have to face your inner slut when it comes to sex.

You can employ a variety of sentence types. Telling your partner how you're feeling and exploring your body's feelings and ideas might be the greatest place to start. Another method of engaging in dirty chat is to express your desires to him, such as how you want to spit, squeeze your nipples, or whisper in your ear. Telling your spouse and getting to know his well-being is the third filthy talk tactic.

Every man desires a woman who is unpredictable and open to trying new things to spice up her relationships, especially in the bedroom, especially when it comes to sex. Are you this kind of girl?

You're happy to have read this, I'm sure. I'm confident these few tips will inspire you to start having naughty conversations with your lover in bed and change the dynamic of your sex life.

a) Analysis of ideas. You're already searching for worthy concepts. You'll understand more about filthy talking once you read other ladies' thoughts, opinions, and posts. Most girls would brush off the idea of nasty conversation as belonging to slutes and porn stars, but isn't that exactly what a man craves in bed?

b) Obtain a handbook for instructions. The easiest way to prevent anything from becoming mixed up is to locate a comprehensive guide, like an eBook, authored by someone with experience in both sex and dirty conversation. An eBook like this will have all the information you require after you learn how to start talking nasty in bed.

b) Rapid start-up. Sigh and murmur encouraging words in your ear; that's the greatest place to start. It is inappropriate to start yelling and screaming since this might be phony and depressing. Uttering phrases like "Oh yes!" and "I'm feeling good. "It's enough to alter his thoughts, feelings, and behaviors.

d) Put what you're seeking into practice. The words you have saved in your thoughts when you are "alone" can be played within your bathroom, and you can even use them for flirting or sexting. Many things you frequently learn over time are combined into dirty talk.

Get to know your man. Get to know your man. He wants you to quit using words or phrases that you know are offensive. Recognize which sentences to use against him and when to use them. Practice your phrases to tell him how you feel, what needs to be done, and what he did right.

You will eventually see how beneficial dirty discussion is for a relationship, even though it may initially seem strange and uncomfortable. Start changing your sex life dramatically tonight by implementing these top 5 suggestions!

Ways To Make Your Physical Appearance Better

A person's physical appearance is a major factor in attracting women. It is crucial to make an effort to maintain proper hygiene and grooming, as well as to dress nicely, even though it is not the sole factor. Here are some tips on how to look better and draw in women:

Keeping up proper hygiene:

This entails taking frequent showers, cleaning your teeth, and applying deodorant. Maintaining good cleanliness enhances your attractiveness to women and demonstrates your self-care.

Put on nice clothes:

This involves dressing in well-fitting, spotless, and occasion-appropriate attire. Take your time choosing clothes that accentuate your best features and give you a sense of self-assurance.

Maintaining your skin's health:

Women find clear, healthy skin appealing. Ensure your skincare regimen is consistent and the items you use are appropriate for your skin type.

Maintaining your hair:

How well-groomed your hair is can significantly impact how beautiful you seem to women. Use the right hair products, get frequent haircuts, and follow your hair care regimen consistently.

Regular exercise:

Frequent exercise enhances your physical appearance, self-esteem, and attractiveness.

Observing your body language: How you appear to women can also be influenced by your body language. Elevate your posture, meet your eyes, and smile. This demonstrates your approachability and confidence.

Being self-assured

It's critical to feel good about your looks, regardless of how you look. Recall that each person is unique, and that charm comes from confidence.

How to Wear the Correct Attire and Accessory Items to Draw Women

Your choice of attire and accessories can greatly influence your appearance to ladies. The following advice will help you select the appropriate attire and accessories to draw in women:

Put on appropriate attire for the situation.

It's crucial to wear clothing that fits the situation. For instance, your attire should alter depending on whether you're heading out on a date or just hanging out with pals.

Fit is crucial.

How appealing you appear to women can be greatly influenced by clothing that fits properly. Ensure your clothing is neither too tight nor loose and fits you comfortably.

You can appear more desirable to ladies by wearing certain colors. For instance, you might wear apparel in red, orange, and yellow tones if your skin tone is warm.

Accoutered

Accessories can give your ensemble a unique flair and individuality. Consider finishing your look with a great pair of shoes, a belt, or a watch.

Try out several styles.

You can obtain the ideal look for you by trying out a variety of designs. Draw inspiration from many style icons, experiment, and choose what suits you best.

Be who you are.

It's critical to choose apparel and accessories that reflect your actual self. Avoid attempting to pass for someone you're not, and refrain from dressing uneasily.

Remain straightforward:

It's typically better to be minimalistic in terms of attire and accessories. Maintain a timeless appearance, and ladies will be drawn to you.

Chapter 3: The Health and Mental Advantages of Increased Sexual Activity

Beyond the benefits it offers you and your partner directly, having regular sex promotes a healthy relationship in many other ways as well. For example, the oxytocin released during sexual activity promotes emotional closeness and a sense of unity. 3.

In a monogamous relationship, having sex increases your level of devotion to your partner and strengthens your emotional bond. When a couple expresses their love through sex, they have a higher chance of staying together. Thus, there is a positive correlation between sex and a lower divorce rate.

Beyond the obvious emotional benefits of having sex, there are several other bodily benefits as well. Several of these include:

● Enhanced physical health: Intercourse is an activity. The American Heart Association compares having sex to moderate physical activity like walking quickly or climbing two flights of stairs.

7. During intercourse, the muscles in the abdomen and pelvis may become tauter and more toned. Women with higher muscle tones are more adept at controlling their bladders.

Enhanced cerebral activity More often occurring sex sessions were linked to improved cognitive function and the growth of new brain cells in early rat studies. Subsequent research on people has demonstrated comparable benefits. Over 6,000 participants in a 2018 study found that regular sex was linked to better memory performance in those over 50.

- Enhanced immunological performance: Increased sex is good for immune system health. Frequent sex may lower your chance of catching a cold or the flu.

- Pain reduction: Endorphins associated with sex have a role in more than just relaxation and happiness. Moreover, it appears that endorphins from sex reduce migraine and back pain.
- Weight loss: 200 calories are burned during a 30-minute sexual session.
- Increased desire and vaginal lubrication from increased sexual activity are two more physical benefits. Less painful cramping and shorter menstrual cycles are associated with regular sexual activity. Additionally, improved digestion, better teeth, glowing skin, and an improved sense of

smell may all be related to the body's release of the hormone DHEA during an orgasm.

The benefits of having sex are numerous. It might promote positive relationships and general well-being. Additionally, it has been connected to benefits for the individual, including lowered stress, improved immunity, improved sleep, and improved cardiac health.

Sex Has Psychological Benefits There are many psychological and emotional benefits of making love (sex is significantly linked to a better quality of life). Among these benefits are: ● Engaging in sexual activity can boost one's sense of self-worth and reduce feelings of insecurity, leading to more positive self-evaluations.

● Higher happiness: A 2015 Chinese study discovered that people are happier when they engage in more consensual and higher-quality sex.

● Stronger bonds: Hormones released from the brain during sexual activity, like endorphins, reduce inflammation and symptoms of depression. Oxytocin, sometimes known as the "hug drug," is released in reaction to stimulation of the nipples and other sexual activities. 5 Oxytocin plays a role in promoting contentment and tranquility.

● Stress relief: Less frequent sex could result from ongoing stress. However, engaging in sexual activity can be a helpful way to decompress. Sexual engagement has long-lasting effects that reduce stress response hormones, including cortisol and adrenaline (epinephrine).

- Better sleep quality: Prolactin, a hormone that promotes sleep, is produced during orgasms.

Other advantages include: 1. Sex strengthens couples' ties

The closeness that arises and is experienced during monogamous sex strengthens commitment, emotional attachments, and ties. According to Maslow's Hierarchy of Needs, it preserves a healthy level of closeness, affection, and belongingness that humans inherently require.

A relationship may get stronger and retain its "spark" through sex. It maintains the resolve to stand by one another in adversity.

Intimacy during sex also builds and fortifies your spouse's support network. Those with robust social networks are often more adept at forming enduring relationships and managing stress.

2. A fulfilling sexual relationship improves mood and happiness

Does science support the idea that having sex strengthens relationships? Yes, it is the solution.

When you are less worried, you will feel happier and more satisfied.

First of all, prolactin is released during an orgasm. Its main function is to aid in lactation, promoting relaxation and sound sleep. Furthermore, a relaxed body can better preserve emotional and physical ties.

Another way to decompress is via sex. This results in reduced secretion of cortisol and adrenaline, which generate physiological stress reactions such as fatigue and raised blood pressure.

The brain also releases feel-good chemicals called endorphins during sexual activity. They minimize loneliness and annoyance while elevating mood.

An additional chemical is released during increased sexual excitement. Its chemical name, oxytocin, promotes calm and contented emotions.

What is oxytocin? For sex and pregnancy, the brain creates this peptide hormone, which the posterior pituitary secretes.

3. Having sex increases self-esteem and respect

Confidence increases as sexual satisfaction increases. This is so because having sex boosts one's confidence.

Then, this may have a favorable and beneficial impact on social connections, especially romantic ones.

As mentioned before, sex increases oxytocin levels in the body, which fosters intimacy. It helps satisfy some of people's emotional demands.

People get more bonded to one another through sex, develop a want for cuddles, and experience the need to hold and be held by others.

4. Sex Promotes Spontaneity in Relationships

One may wonder what role sexual closeness plays in a committed relationship.

There's always a feeling of excitement when there's something new to look forward to. The same is true about sex.

Improving your in-bed romance can contribute to a more passionate and romantic relationship. Couples feel more secure in their commitment to one another as a result.

5. Rekindling love is one of the many benefits of having sex in marriage and committed partnerships.

By encouraging spouses to actively engage in love behaviors despite hectic schedules and demanding duties, sex can strengthen relationships. It brings two people back together and puts them in the discovery phase, allowing them to grow as people and a couple.

Add Your Own Principles And Beliefs.

Overview

Any discussion you have with your child about sex and sexuality must take your principles and values into account. First, you should share your principles and values with your child while talking to them about birds and bees.

In this manner, you can be certain that your child will understand the situation better. For this reason, you should help them make the best decisions by providing excellent life advice.

Here are a few effective and helpful ways to converse with your child about birds and bees. These suggestions make it easy to explain to your child the real world of sex and have a conversation about it.

How to Have a Useful and Effective Conversation with Your Child About Sex

Ensure you have enough references to start your debate and don't forget to highlight your values and views. A parent who upholds strong moral principles can be of great assistance to their child in navigating challenges related to sex and sexuality.

Get over your humiliation.

It makes sense if the phrases "penis" and "vagina" initially make you uncomfortable. You should repeat these words to yourself several times until you feel confident enough to talk about them calmly with your child and get over your embarrassment. If you do this, you'll find that talking to your child about sex makes you feel more relaxed and at ease. One of the best ways to swiftly overcome your shame is to schedule regular, honest conversations with your child.

Make time for regular, honest conversations with your youngster.

Scholars agree that it's vital to teach your child about sex and sexuality, especially while they're young. But it's equally crucial that you keep teaching them about this topic as they get older. For the rest of their lives, your child will deal with issues related to sex and sexuality, and it might be challenging to cover everything in one talk. After you and your child have finally created an open line of communication, let the facts speak for themselves and let the dispute play out. Make the most of your chances to learn. For example, when you and your child see a pregnant woman or hear about sexual incidents on the news. These teaching moments can facilitate smooth transitions into conversations about sexual predicaments.

Thus, educational moments will help you to facilitate conversations about sex, especially when your child gets older and more mature.

Make sure your kids are aware of the facts.

One of the best morals and values a parent should have is knowing the facts about sex and getting precise information and details about sex.

In recent years, extensive sexual data has been made publicly accessible on the internet. You can also provide age-appropriate reading materials for your youngster. You might tell your youngster you'll check into it and get back to them if they ask you a question you don't know the answer to.

Give Your Youngster Specific Information

After your child has experienced nocturnal emissions and menstruation for a few months, it is not a good idea to explain these things to them. The first topic you should discuss with your child concerning sexual experiences and puberty stages is before they reach puberty. If you do this, you'll find that your child is less interested in their body and what's happening to it.

Avoid lecturing

Since today's kids don't want to be lectured, refrain from lecturing. The best thing you can do is to have in-depth conversations about the topic and supply sufficient knowledge and statistics. Although your child will make their own decisions about sex, it is crucial that you, as a parent, give them particular information and resources to help them make well-informed decisions. Without a doubt, discussions and debates will benefit your child more than lectures. Additionally, you may be confident that your child will listen to you and what you say.

Inform Them About the Dangers and Pleasures of Sex

Studies show that having sex is not a bad thing in life, so you shouldn't be afraid of it. Conversely, some individuals think that having sex can be risky. Real-life sex is beautiful and natural, which is one of the reasons your child needs to have solid knowledge and comprehension of sex.

They also have a right to know the basics of sexuality and sex and how to manage these responsibilities in their lives. Conversation with your child about intimacy and relationships will greatly help them understand this subject. You can be sure that your child will have a solid understanding of sex if you, as a parent, get in touch with them as soon as possible.

Section Three
Men's Perspectives on Sexuality
Men enjoy sex because it gives them physical pleasure, which is how they originally viewed it. This is also the reason why they prefer having sex over other relationship-related activities, in contrast to women.

Smell and sight appeal to men, and they are all bodily stimuli.

Men and women can both have orgasms, but they do so in very different ways. Orgasms are shorter and more intense in men, and like other components of sex, they are more focused on the body.

The following observations are made about how men perceive sex:

Men consider having sex. Many times

The majority of men under 60 think about having sex at least once a day, compared to only 25% of women. And that's not all. Compared to women, men have sex fantasies far more frequently and in a wider variety. In addition, they think about casual sex more than women do. But thinking and doing are two different things.

Men value sex.

It's a fallacy that most men think sex is just sex. Many people view having sex as a vital act between two committed people. Males also find that the most rewarding sexual relationship is with a committed partner, just like most women do. One explanation is that long-term partners are more adept at pacifying one another than outsiders.

Not all men are ready for sex.

To the surprise of many women, guys aren't always in the mood for sex—contrary to what was previously said in this book. Just like women, men also encounter stress from work, family, and financial obligations. Additionally, stress dramatically lowers libido. That a guy isn't interested in you tonight doesn't always mean it's untrue. They're just saying that they don't want to have sex at that moment.

Males like to see their partners pleased.

Your man is interested in your feelings for him. They will know what you want unless you tell them. Too many women are uncomfortable voicing their preferences. If you can communicate with them clearly and in a way that doesn't offend them, they'll listen. Since they know that if you're happy, they will also be.

Men tend to wander when their desires aren't satisfied.

If a man feels unloved and undervalued in his relationship, he could seek fulfillment elsewhere. For one man, that can mean losing himself in his profession. Sports or video games can cause someone else to develop an obsession. Some men lie as well. To avoid this, partners must work together to satisfy one another's desires.

Verification of sexual orientation

Sometimes, a man's sexual encounters with other people are more about him than they are about her.

Specializing in adult education, Amanda Pasciucco states that "for some men, sex is a validation of how good-looking they are – if they're having sex with someone they see as better looking than them, for example."

Sex for affirmation or "conquest" usually occurs during the passion stage if he wants to feel strong, attractive, or desirable.

Using sex to connect and feel comfortable

For most men, having sex with a partner is a means of bonding. Put another way, a man's desire for sex with his partner during the stages of attraction and attachment may be motivated by a desire to build a closer relationship with them.

Infidelity in sexual matters

A man may cheat on his wife for a variety of reasons, one of which is that he wants to rekindle their romance while their passion is at its highest and their sex is simple and new.

According to Prause, those who have little sexual satisfaction in their existing relationship are rarely likely to engage in non-monogamous sexual activity.

Those who have an unfaithful partner are likely to be more likely than others to do those things if given the chance, although not everyone who is predisposed to them does. A study suggests that men may find monogamy less difficult than women—indeed, the opposite may be true.

We believe that men struggle more with monogamy than women do only because it has historically and culturally been more acceptable for men to explore and act on a desire for more sexual diversity.

Is That True, Sweetheart?

From a developmental standpoint, it does take a certain amount of emotional intelligence and maturity to recognize true love and know when you've found it. We don't spend much time or effort teaching our children how to recognize love, which is one of the main reasons teens (and maybe many adults) need a lot of "Love 101." This means that many of our young people will start relationships thinking they are in love only to find out later on—often the hard way—that they weren't in love. We must work hard to teach our kids about love, including what it is and how to spot it.

Yes, there are a lot of strong emotions and feelings in the world that resemble love. Many have found that the early attitudes, emotions, and behaviors frequently associated with love in a relationship are insufficient to establish true, long-lasting love. Our previous perception of love was nothing more than lust, passion, or infatuation. Does that sound familiar to you? You can probably think of a few situations in which you thought you were truly in love, only to find out later that it wasn't true love. Those feelings may have led you to make decisions that, in retrospect, weren't in your best interests. Since many adults struggle to recognize true love when they experience it, we can only imagine how tough it must be for young people.

Our children find it far more difficult to navigate the love dilemma than many of us and far more so than our parents and grandparents. They act in this way because their society has a disproportionately high number of sexually active youth and young adults. Furthermore, matters become considerably more complex when sex is involved than when a relationship hasn't progressed that far. Because of this, the issue of young people misidentifying love is far more significant now than when many of us were younger. Unlike children of previous generations, children of today could think they are in love and get very near to having intimate sexual relations.

Additionally, the likelihood of encountering a sexual risk situation—such as pregnancy, sexual assault, STDs, etc.—increases with proximity to sexual activity. Because of this, a big part of our job as parents is to help our kids realize how hard it is to find true love and learn the skills to distinguish true love from other kinds of romantic relationships. I hope you now see how important it is to focus on defining love in your attempts to be approachable for your kids. Love should be the foundation for all the many teachings about sexuality that we hope to impart to our children as they mature.

A Heartfelt Companion

I often bring up friendships as part of a bigger conversation about sexuality with kids at different school levels. After all these years, I tell fourth- and fifth-graders that I still believe in my wife, and then I ask them about their friends. I think a good way to help kids comprehend love is to ask them to consider what makes their best friends different from their regular ones. The following is how the conversation goes:

How many times have you drifted apart from a friend over something they did that you found objectionable?

One child says, "Well, my friend once lied to me." Some state that "mine blamed me for something bad that she did," while others add, "My friend stole five dollars from me; I couldn't believe it."

I ask again, "How many of you have a best friend?" The majority of hands are up. What sets a best friend apart from a casual or everyday friend?

The students gave various answers but insisted that there was a big difference. One said, "You know your best friend much longer and much better than regular friends." Another responds, "They are always there for you, and you can always rely on them." "You can always trust them; they wouldn't hurt you."

The children's answers to this question are invariably spot-on. Your closest friend is the one who has known you the longest. He and you are in a relationship. Looking back over a significant amount of time, you can see that the closest friend wouldn't lie to you, wouldn't give you the truth, and wouldn't do something that was meant to hurt you. Now that you've known your best buddy for a time, you are in a much better position to evaluate them. It will be simpler to assess how excellent of a buddy he is the longer it goes without a negative incident. Regular friends are not the same as best friends. Teaching kids what it takes to become—and stay—best friends with someone is essential to helping them realize when they have found love, respect, and trust in a romantic relationship.

After discussing the differences between friends and best friends, I returned to my husband's narrative. I tell the students that my spouse and I became great friends before we were married and have stayed that way ever since. Whether I force myself to have sex with him or refuse, I never have to worry that he will injure me. My spouse and I truly love, respect, and trust each other. Everyone should be in a relationship with someone who has a past like this before having sex.

How can you tell when someone loves, respects, and believes in you?

One of the biggest problems in life is finding a mate who possesses these wonderful and endearing qualities. Nobody is great at recognizing when they have all of these qualities in a relationship; there are probably many people out there who got married believing they had all of these qualities only to later get divorced. However, I know that as parents, we could devote more time to teaching our children the value of respect, love, and trust. Furthermore, we shouldn't rely on our schools to help with instruction of this kind. There are likely no real "love, respect, and trust experts" out there, but common sense dictates that if we give our kids enough time to explore these qualities in meaningful and wise ways, they'll be far more likely to recognize the real deal when they see it. Thus, please talk to your kids about love, respect, and trust as much as possible.

Real-World Instances of Love, Respect, and Trust

This one is very simple: just spend some time demonstrating to your child what real-life love, respect, and trust are like. Discuss it with your child when your partner or spouse behaves in a way that exemplifies any of these traits. Remember to let your children know when you observe your neighbors and acquaintances exhibiting these characteristics. Even if your child is watching a movie or television show with you and one of them is portrayed, bring it up to their notice. You want your youngster to cherish the "big three" qualities in any loving and encouraging relationship; real-life examples don't have to involve sexuality. Then, when it's convenient, go back to one of these examples and emphasize how important these characteristics are, especially in a sexual relationship.

As your child gains reference points for the big three, she will become increasingly skilled at identifying them when she comes across them. Any examples you can think of will help, but try to focus on those that exemplify the three key elements of real romantic relationships: someone going above and beyond out of love for their partner, someone sacrificing a personal desire out of consideration for his partner's wishes, or someone letting go of something that requires a significant amount of trust.

For example, if your spouse's friend stays at a female coworker's apartment because he worked late and the commute is too long, you can talk to your friend about how she needs to trust her husband not to "fool around." If you know someone who agreed to put off having children for a while so that their partner could go to college and start a career, you can talk to your child about how much his partner must love him. When a friend vehemently disagrees with her partner's belief that their seventeen-year-old son shouldn't be allowed to have friends around while they are out for the night, you can discuss how to respect your partner's stance.

Obstacles to successful sexual communication

Even in the closest of partnerships, having a candid conversation about sexual concerns can be challenging. Numerous things, including fear of being judged, humiliated, ignorance, cultural differences, gender norms, and power imbalances, may be to blame. We will go into great detail about each of these obstacles in this conversation and provide solutions.

1. Fear of Judgment: Individuals may be reluctant to discuss their sexual sensations and ideas for fear of their partner passing judgment.

2. Embarrassment: Talking about sexual matters can make people feel awkward and ashamed.

3. Lack of Knowledge: Some people may be unfamiliar with the jargon and vocabulary used when discussing sexual issues.

4. Cultural differences: People may find it awkward to talk about sexual matters because of cultural standards and beliefs.

5. Gender Roles: Conventional gender roles might make one or both partners uncomfortable when discussing sex honestly and openly.

6. Power differentials: Individuals in unequal partnerships could feel that they can't be completely honest and

upfront about their sexual needs and desires.

Communication problems about gender

The difficulties that develop when men and women try to interact with one another are referred to as gender communication issues. Power dynamics, linguistic barriers, and gender roles are only a few causes of these difficulties.

Gender roles can exert a noteworthy influence on the communication styles of both genders. Men would be expected, for instance, to initiate discussion and be assertive, whereas women might be expected to be more accommodating and subservient. When trying to communicate, this may cause misunderstandings and frustrations.

Communication problems might also arise from linguistic differences. Miscommunication can occur when men and women use different words and phrases to convey the same concepts. For instance, a male may be attempting to be straightforward with a woman when he says something that comes off as hostile.

Power dynamics can also influence the way that men and women communicate. Men could be perceived as having greater authority and might be less receptive to women's opinions. When trying to communicate, this might make women feel devalued and unheard.

Communication problems might also result from cultural expectations and customs. Misunderstandings may arise because, for instance, men and women may have different expectations of the nature of conversations.

Understanding the contributing causes of gender communication challenges is crucial to resolving them. Men and women can collaborate to produce a more productive and courteous conversation by being aware of the many gender roles, linguistic variations, power dynamics, and cultural conventions that might impact communication.

Ways to Get Rid of Shyness

It could be difficult to put your deepest sexual sentiments into words if you are a timid person or if you tend to be reserved when it comes to sexual expression. However, you are not by yourself. No matter how long they've been with their partners, even extroverts often struggle to communicate their sexual wants to others.

Here are a few short tips that will help you get over your shyness and express your thoughts during foreplay and sex.

Have A Deep Conversation With Your Significant Other.

If you are honest with your lover about wanting to spice up your sex life, they will probably love and respect you more. You only have to tell them that you're timid and nervous about the concept of being more forthcoming during sex but that you wish you could be more forthcoming with words. To take the chance to experiment without fear, guilt, or shame, enlist your partner's support. This conversation can be used to establish limits and find out what the two of you enjoy and dislike.

You can significantly reduce your fear and anxiety related to vulgar conversation by taking this first step.

But it doesn't instantly make you a fearless, obscene speaker. It is still necessary for you to open your mouth and let the words come out naturally. Remind yourself that you have your partner's loving support if fear, guilt, or shame prevent you from moving forward. Breathe deeply and release yourself. Even if you must whisper what you're saying, give yourself permission to connect with your feelings and desires and express them verbally. Don't allow fear to prevent you from expressing your true self and being accepted for who you are without self-censorship.

The most important thing is to get beyond the initial obstacle. You will experience levels of sexual intimacy and bliss you never imagined possible after you get over it. Additionally, you will feel more confident in practically every area of your life, improving your relationship. Make use of sounds.

Using groaning sounds (oh, ah, yes, mmm, ugghh, and so on) might help you ease into talking nasty. Gain self-assurance in utilizing sound to demonstrate your presence with your spouse during stressful situations. Once you feel at ease expressing yourself verbally through groans, you can whisper random words and phrases into your partner's ear. They are not required to understand what you are saying. To increase their perception of sexual pleasure during foreplay or intercourse, just whisper anything - anything - in their ears.

Make use of brief sentences.

If you are shy or new to dirty talk, you could find it very challenging to put together a long statement. Continue using brief sentences or one-liners. As an illustration, consider the following: deeper, faster, slower, don't stop, and so on. All of them are straightforward expressions that might enhance sexual pleasure without being offensive or explicit. Short sentences like "I need you now," "Touch me softly," "Hold me tight," "Tonight, I'm all yours," and so on can also be used as foreplay.

Proceed to the descriptive sentences.

Once your confidence has grown, you can use more detailed language to express to your partner how you feel, what you need from them, or even what you want done to them. For instance, "I love how you kiss me passionately," "It feels so good when you do that," "I enjoy pleasing you," "I wish we would never stop," "I want your lips all over my body," or "I want to melt into you."

Once more, there's no need to jump right into these topics or try to incorporate every kind of dirty talk into a single or few conversations. You have lots of time and opportunity to explore, modify, and advance your abilities. Don't limit your sensual conversations to just during sex if you want to assist yourself in getting over your shyness even more. You have all day to rehearse and maintain the desire to have sex with your spouse. Remember that having sex shouldn't necessarily follow nasty talk. You can have fun talking to Shady simply by yourself.

Employ text messaging

If you enjoy the notion of talking nasty but are too bashful to even bring yourself to groan aloud, try texting your lover something sexy to see how it feels. Speaking with them virtually will make it a little simpler for you to express yourself. Once you've finished writing your letter, hit submit quickly to avoid letting doubt, fear, or your overly modest side get the better of you.

Whenever your spouse enjoys your text message, you will gradually build the courage to express these words in person.

By taking up this book, you've already done the first step, but let's also get your head in the game. Please consider the sexiest thing you can envision. Don't be afraid to express your filthy views.

Let's now concentrate on your mate. What particular aspect of them irritates you the most? When was the last time you got caught up in a book? What action did they take to make you feel divine? Have you told them how much you cherished it? Express your enjoyment to them with your body language, sounds, and words.

Let's be even more precise now. Consider the sexual act itself. What is the best thing about spending time with your partner? Consider their physique and the reasons it appeals to you so much. What sounds do they make that most arouse your interest? Remember that they have specific preferences as well. What are they? Imagine every element in rich, thrilling detail.

Some ladies can be a little hesitant when it comes to nasty talk. I was once in a relationship with a woman who was afraid to disclose her true feelings. However, with some support and direction, she began to open up and let her filthy ideas out.

We discussed her favorite things to do for sex with her partner and what made her feel most attracted to him. We investigated the sounds and words from her spouse that caused her heart to race. By the conclusion, she felt more assured and anxious to try out some new nasty words in the bedroom.

Let your dirty ideas run wild and see where they lead you—after all, everything begins in the mind.

You see, the first step toward becoming at ease with obscene discourse is mental. Therefore, let's align your thinking, and then we may proceed accordingly.

How To Quit Worrying Too Much About What To Say In Bed

Are you preoccupied with what to say during sex time and caught in a loop in your mind? Do you shudder at the mere notion of saying the wrong thing? Overthinking can ruin the mood and throw off your joy train, but there are techniques to escape this mental cage. In this chapter, we will drop some tasty tips and methods to help you fly your freak flag and speak your truth.

First and foremost, it's critical to keep in mind that having sexual pleasure depends heavily on communication. Communicating your requirements and desires to your spouse is important because they are not mind readers. But how can one accomplish that without going overboard?

Concentrating on your senses is one method. Pay attention to how your body feels and the sensations you're experiencing rather than stressing about what to say. Next, verbalize those emotions as they arise. Express your happiness with your spouse by letting them know, whether with a gasp, a sigh, or a moan.

Another piece of advice is to start with straightforward yet impactful praises. Tell your lover how much you like their touch or how attracted you are to them. These compliments can help you become more self-assured and provide your spouse with a sense of appreciation and desire.

Try lightening the mood with a little comedy if you're still feeling stuck. Don't be scared to joke around or playfully taunt your spouse to defuse a tense situation. Laughing may be a very effective icebreaker and relaxant for the group.

And never forget that it's acceptable to fumble over your words or appear uncomfortable. Maintaining open channels of communication and perseverance are crucial. Speaking up during sex grows easier and more natural with experience.

To be present, take a deep breath, let go of any overanalyzing, and release yourself. You'll be shocked at how much more gratifying and pleasurable the experience may be when you're not always thinking about it.

I used to constantly second-guess my words in bed. I was afraid I might say something stupid or inappropriate. However, it was detracting from the encounter and our relationship.

I decided to quit overthinking and put some of the advice and methods I had learned into practice. I began by concentrating on my partner and the message I wanted to give them. They were with me because they wanted to be, I told myself, and they were interested in what I had to say.

I also worked on some positive self-talk and self-affirmation to increase my confidence. I convinced myself that I was attractive and sensual and that my words carried as much weight as my deeds.

Furthermore, what do you know? It was successful! I was able to speak without overanalyzing and to let my words flow. I was even taken aback by how assured and seductive I sounded. It truly brought our sex life to a whole new level of closeness and pleasure.

I don't think about what to say during sex anymore. My boyfriend enjoys it when I just follow my gut and my wants. The impact that letting go of the over-analysis can have is incredible.

Section Three

Assume nothing too high.

It's scary, for whatever reason, to tell our spouse what we want to try, quit, or modify in our sex life. A qualified clinical psychologist named Dr. Mimi Shagaga says that initially, feeling anxious is quite natural. According to Dr.Shagaga, "Sex can be a taboo subject for many."A lot of the time, it has to do with how sex was or wasn't talked about in our childhood/family of origin. It can also be a touchy subject if you have any insecurities about your sexuality or body image.

Select a moment when you feel at ease and ease.

"Take a break and ask your partner first, 'I want to talk to you about some of the ways I'd like to explore our sex life.

Don't try to talk to them during or right after sex because that's when we're most vulnerable and might misunderstand. Make sure you talk to them when both of you are calm, and there are no distractions. Is now the right moment?"" Bourquin uttered.

Boquin has offered some basic discussion starters to get you started if you're unsure how to approach the topic:

"How do you feel about our current sexual life?"

"What is the extent of your enjoyment of our sexual life?"

What is your favorite aspect of our sexual life?"

What was your biggest concern about my reaction? Is there anything about your sexual wants that you were reluctant to share?

"I like it when _ during sex."

"Is it okay if I tell you about the several things I would like to explore with you?"

"How can I make it safer for us to talk freely about sex?"

According to Bourquin, reminding your partner of his wonderful qualities is the simplest method to ensure that he doesn't feel threatened. Start the conversation by talking about the aspects of your sexual life that you enjoy and wish to keep going, and then on to talk about the things you would like to alter.

"It's important to communicate with your partner your likes and dislikes," stated Dr.Shagaga. "While this can be a difficult conversation, the right partner will be open and receptive to that communication."

How to approach the things you wish to alter

Expressing your demands and desires is critical if you believe they aren't being satisfied. First, identify the needs that aren't being met for you and stick with them, advises Bourquin. For instance, your partner leaves before letting you have an orgasm and thinks the sexual activity has ended. Or perhaps you both enjoy oral sex, but your spouse is afraid to attempt it. Nothing is too tiny or too huge to discuss with someone we have sex with—the possibilities are boundless. Be honest and upfront about what you are missing, and at that point, Bourquin advises asking your spouse if they're comfortable receiving feedback. If they say yes, "put it down." "Don't blame your partner; just share what you would love more and what it would mean to you if you had more," Bourquin advised. Would you be willing to hear some ways you could help me meet more of these needs? Bourquin suggests asking questions along the lines of, "Is it okay if I share with you something that weighs heavily on me in our sex life? I realized that I would like/want more of _, and it's been frustrating not having that need met."

Bourquin continued, saying you shouldn't leave a relationship because your partner can't fulfill your requirements.

How do you tell your partner when you want to try something new?

You can achieve the desired outcomes by telling your spouse about the wild, fantastical sex dream you had a few nights before. Still, if they require more encouragement, Boquin suggests saying, "So I have this fantasy about _ What do you want to think?" Is this something we can explore together?"

How to carry on the discussion later

Well, you've told your partner what you want to try, and everything seems good. But now what? Dr.Shagaga clarified that being truthful is crucial in all areas of your relationship. Try something new that you've been discussing and don't like. Or rather, do you love it? Tell them!" She said.

A professor who specializes in sex, love, and relationships, Justin Lehmiller, argues that having sex is one of the most intimate and life-affirming things you can do with someone, but talking about it is far harder. "You're much more vulnerable to talking about sex than having it," he adds.

The good news is that experts think opening up can make you happier at every stage of your life and will benefit your sex life.

A couple coming to me with a sexual problem, it's rarely about that one thing. For example, someone with low desire may hold a grudge about something else for twenty years. Poor communication about sex "is often a sign that you're miscommunicating about everything," says psychosexual and relationship therapist Krystal Woodbridge.

Is it ever a bad idea to discuss sex with your partner? Cate Campbell, a psychosexual therapist and couples counselor, says that it's never a good idea to criticize your partner's performance. Lehmiller advises you to always gauge your partner's comfort level and avoid discussing potentially threatening topics.

Here are some pointers to help you make your sexual talk as fruitful, informative, and pleasurable as possible. So, where do you begin?

Get started now

"Build trust and intimacy first with simpler conversations, such as about consent or contraception," advises Lehmiller. "You can then move on to what feels good to you and what doesn't and go from there." The longer you wait, the harder it gets to talk about sex.

"Start slow and take it slow," he advises when it comes to revealing fantasies. "Start with tame vanilla fantasies to see how your partner reacts." This will foster intimacy and trust. In a committed relationship, you have plenty of time together. Let them know what part they play in your fantasy to ensure that your spouse doesn't feel excluded or intimidated.

... yet there's always time to get started.

"If years or decades have gone by without a couple talking about sex, I often suggest an amnesty," adds Woodbridge. He advises couples to act like they've never met before, saying, "I tell them, forget all that came before." This makes it easier for them to concentrate on their goals for the future rather than the past. According to Campbell, elderly adults who did not grow up with tools may find communicating difficult. "When a person is 'rebooting' later in life, perhaps after a divorce or the death of a partner, I encourage them to have a good conversation about their expectations before jumping into bed with someone new."

Allow your fantasies to come to you.

Only half of us have sexual fantasies, according to Lehmiller, who polled over 4,000 people for his 2018 book Tell Me What You Want. People find it difficult to disclose these desires. However, there are numerous benefits to doing this. "People who talk about their fantasies report the happiest sex," according to him. "But there's a lot of shame around her."

97% of fantasies, according to Lehmiller's research, may be broadly categorized into the following: non-monogamous sex, deeper emotional connection, novelty and adventure, rough sex, sex with several partners, voyeurism, and fetishes, and gender flexibility. He declares, "We are more normal than we think." Whether or not we play out our fantasies, sharing them is a simple way to add something new to our sex lives. It can also be thrilling to just express it.

What Are The Advantages Of Tantric Practice?

Health benefits: The tantric massage encourages cleansing and purification. As a result, harmful components are removed from your system. It has been demonstrated that tantric sex has healing and therapeutic potential. Tantra's regenerative power will improve your skin, brain, and other essential organs when you make it a habit to practice these rituals.

Learn about who you are; many people don't even know what they want from life. They are merely living in survival mode and waltzing from day to day. Tantric rituals assist you in discovering your life's purpose and gaining a clear awareness of who you are. These customs also provide you the strength to pursue your goals.

Creativity: Tantric rituals contribute to cultivating an environment that fosters creativity. It has been demonstrated that the full-body orgasm enhances the lovers' mental clarity and fosters their creativity.

Patience is a key component of most tantric rituals; thus, consistently engaging in these practices will help you develop your patience.

Feel good about yourself; tantric practices are the simplest path to happiness and contentment. You can purge yourself of the harmful energy obstructing your tranquility with Tantra. Especially during tantric sex, you get a full-body orgasm that boosts your confidence and ability to enjoy yourself.

Reduces stress: By using different tantric rituals, your body releases tension and old wounds stored in your tissues, revitalizing your entire body. Tantric practices are capable of reducing stress. Tantra relieves stress, enabling you to live a fulfilling and meaningful life.

Increases focus; people who practice Tantra don't put boundaries on themselves. They belong to the collective psyche. Therefore, anything they desire is available for them to take. Tantric rituals help you focus by first getting rid of unnecessary distractions and then by fostering a supportive internal environment. This aids in your goal-achieving.

Stable relationships: getting to know oneself might help you get to know the other. Tantric rituals remove egocentrism and allow you to perceive other people as integral parts of yourself, enhancing your understanding of yourself and others. This mentality enables you to value people for who they are, fostering wonderful relationships. Tantric sex is a personal experience that strengthens a couple's bond.

Section Six

The best way to EDUCATE YOUR KIDS about divorce

Once, two perceptive parents put their preschooler down to explain to him that they would soon be leaving. Gently and carefully, they informed him that although Daddy and Mommy intended to move out and live in different houses, he would still see them regularly. They finished with the most important mark, which was that his parents still loved him, and they asked if he had any questions.

The child, four, remained silent. "Who will take care of me?" he asked afterward.

This short narrative, told by Californian therapist, mediator, and author Joan B. Kelly, provides insight into the differences between adult and child experiences of being apart. These guardians had taken all reasonable precautions. They sought expert advice and tried to provide their child with the basics without being too controlling. But they failed to mention this crucial point, which, although it seemed obvious to them, was not obvious to him.

Adults view it as the complex, multifaceted situation that it is. Typically, young children will see it in tangible and self-centered ways. Understanding where children are at, formatively, will help you support them in adjusting to the reality of separation. Higher perspective consolation will mean almost little to a kid wondering, "Where will the feline live?"

1. Guidelines for having conversations with young children (0–5) regarding distinct, Important formative issues

I. Babies and children

- dependence on parents or other guardians
- Inability to comprehend their feelings, anticipate future events or decipher complicated situations

Ii. Children in preschool

- beginning to encourage independence, but still very dependent
- little ability to understand situations and logical conclusions; still unable to anticipate future events
- Understanding the world revolves around oneself

The boundary between a dream and reality might occasionally be hazy.

- the ability to consider emotions but a limited ability to express them

When Mark Fraser and Mary separated last autumn, their two children, Andrew, then six, and Caitlyn, then four, were used to spending most of their time with Dad because their mother's job kept her away from them other than a few days a month. It, therefore, took Caitlyn some time to adjust to Mary moving out of their Milton, Ontario, home. Even though they had only recently parted ways with their mother, Caitlyn exclaimed, "Mom home?" as the kids got home from their most treasured end-of-week visit. Caitlyn will need to invest and get a lot of fundamental explanations before she can understand.

2. What to check for Preschoolers' nervousness is one of the signs of pain.

Anger or unsteadiness near home could be represented by persistence, trepidation, whining, or general irritability. Additionally, preschoolers could fall behind in their sequence of events. For example, toddlers sleeping through the sunset would wake up more frequently.

Long-term residents may develop false beliefs about the reasons behind and effects of separation due to their limited mental capacity, according to Rhonda Freeman, director of Families in Transition, a program of Toronto's

Family Services Association. "In the event that Dad's the person who leaves the home, they could think, 'Father left me,' as opposed to 'Father left Mom,'" she explains. "Kids need to comprehend that the choice to live separated is a grown-up choice. It's challenging for preschoolers to figure out that."

Parental needs: Children feel secure and comforted when their needs are consistently met and nurtured. As much as is reasonable, toddlers' lives should be protected by their regular routines (dinner, play, bath, and bed) under the supervision of a parent who is "there for them." This is important for all children, especially after a breakup. According to Joan Kelly, "If things aren't working out in a good way at home, juveniles and youngsters can escape by spending time with companions. Children, babies, and preschoolers can't."

Preschoolers require clear, thorough explanations. Follow the basics:

Decide which parent is going out, where the child will live, who will look after him, and how often he will visit the other parent.

Be prepared for inquiries; provide succinct answers when necessary, then pause to see if anything more comes up.

Aim for a few brief ones instead of assuming the work should be completed in a single conversation.

- A little greater ability to reflect and talk about feelings
- A broader, less self-centered viewpoint on the world around them, yet a limited understanding of perplexing situations like separation
- expanding the number of relationships (friends and school) outside the home

Ii. Children aged 9 to 11

- an increased ability to understand, consider, and talk about the feelings and circumstances associated with distinct
- Relationships with others outside the family, such as friends, teachers, and mentors, have become increasingly important in determining how a child spends their time.

• will typically have a clear perspective; blame for divide

Toronto resident Erica Hallman* examines her kindergarten-aged daughter Jessica to understand the arguments underlying her parents' divorce. This assumption was successfully dispelled when she asked, "Is this because he erased something from your PC? For what reason would you say you are battling?" However, Hallman saw from her girl's question that Jessica needed to have some understanding of things she didn't fully understand.

4. Signs that a child has reached school maturity: anxiety and fear

upset or trouble, while some show even more overt signs of longing for their absent guardian. Some people may dream of compromising and can't stop wondering how they may accomplish that. According to Freeman, "Youngsters who imagine that they could possibly unite their folks back, or that they some way or another added to the separation, will experience difficulty continuing ahead with the mending system. So they need to comprehend that those are grown-up choices which they didn't cause and can't impact."

Parental needs: Consistent attention and timetables are still important. Children above this age range are more comfortable talking about their emotions. However, just because they can does not imply they will have to. Books about separation can also help mess with zeroing in on their feelings. Moving toward the point by implication can also be helpful; saying, "A few children feel miserable, apprehensive or even irate when their folks separate" is less undermining than asking directly, "Are you feeling miserable?"

Detailed guidelines for having conversations about the following with children aged 12 to 14: Important formative issues

• a more notable capacity to understand problems related to different

- the beginnings of a desire for further independence; the handling of parental authority
- increasingly important relationships with people outside of the family

When Eve Roseanne Young Men was ten and twelve years old, she went through a messy divorce from her drunken husband. At one point, the designated authority asked the two guardians not to look into the court proceedings because the situation had become so bad. Although it's challenging to shield kids from this kind of conflict entirely, Rosanne tried her best. "I just attempted to make our home a refuge... customary eating times, normal sleep times, and my better half was never permitted in the house. At the point when I left the young men to go out at night, I took my cellphone and advised them to consider me any time." And they frequently called. Joe, her eldest child, started having headaches and had trouble falling asleep. Roseanne: "Given my stress, I was worried that I wouldn't be able to provide him with the adapting skills he needed, so I sought assistance." Joe started visiting a guide who could have been useful to him.

Section Two
How to Look Like You in Less Than a Minute
This isn't Jedi-Mind Tricks 101; this is just plain psychology.

Before attempting to woo women, you should perform a few basic exercises. To start with the basics, these activities include showering and dressing professionally.

Since appearance and scent are the first things women will notice about you, make sure you look and smell good.

After giving yourself a good wash and shower, comb through your hair if it's long enough.

Similarly, launder your garments. Steer clear of expensive, brand-new apparel purchases. Dress impeccably. That's the first step towards winning a woman over.

When you first meet a lady, you can instantly win her with a clever move I invented.

To create a woman similar to you, THIS SYSTEM DOES NOT RELY ON THE WORDS YOU SAY.

Conversely, it's how you seem, both literally and figuratively. Let me explain.

It takes less than two seconds for someone to establish an opinion about you.

According to a Harvard School of Health Sciences study, participants were asked to assess a professor's likeability and personality based on a two-second video clip, and the results showed that this was true.

Despite having only two minutes with the professor, these students came to the same conclusions as those in his class the entire semester.

What conclusions may be drawn from this study?

I find this to be evidence of how frequently we make snap decisions.

To be successful in dating, you have to realize that in the first two seconds of meeting someone, you genuinely form an opinion about how likable they are.

When we like someone, we usually see the best in them.

Again, we see the best side of them.

A woman will determine she likes you and wants to know more about you in the first two seconds of meeting you.

At this point, you're probably wondering how to rapidly win them over.

We respond to the attitude and body language you project.

Your demeanor influences how others read your nonverbal clues.

Use the LSO System to win her over after you're in the right mindset.

Put another way, to look, smile, and open up your body.

1. Observe

Make eye contact with a woman when you first meet her. This shows that you are a gentleman and conveys confidence. Staring down instead of staring someone in the eye when you first meet them in Western society is a sign of submission to your discussion partner. You are automatically downgraded as a result.

Similarly, when you turn away from your conversation partner during a conversation, you are sending an implicit message that they are unimportant to you or that you are only giving them half of your attention.

A disdainful attitude is not going to get the desired results.

This information is rather basic when we break it down, but it's important to remember these principles because we often forget them when we're under pressure to perform well.

This is much more likely to happen when we first meet someone we like and find attractive. It's critical to establish a good impression.

Make direct eye contact with her.

2. GRIND

Nicholas Boothman asks, "Are you charming or alarming? When we first meet someone, we categorize them as either excellent or terrible."

Smiling is one of the best ways to appear approachable and non-threatening.

This brings us to our third point: being transparent.

3. ENSHROLL YOUR LANGUAGE

You're standing guarded and protective when you cross your arms in front of someone; you're building a mental and physical wall between the two of you.

This is not something you want to say.

You want to assert that I'm dependable and honest. You do this by opening your chest.

The best way to develop a trusting attitude is to show your heart. You should position your heart to face the other person's heart when communicating.

This is how dogs show you how much they trust them: they come to you, lay on their backs, and let you rub their stomachs.

Similarly, you are requesting interaction from a woman when you show her your chest and heart, which tells her that you are reliable and honest.

That's it, friends—a guide on how to wow a woman in the first two, not the first ten seconds of meeting her!

Remember LSO: Look a woman in the eyes, smile, and open your body and ideas.

Boothman says that your strength comes from your capacity to change your mindset. These three easy methods can help you approach a woman with a positive outlook and win her over.

Typical Blunders Males Make When Speaking With Women

Men occasionally make blunders when communicating with women, resulting in miscommunications and unfavorable encounters. If males are aware of these typical communication errors and take action to fix them, they can be easily avoided.

Men frequently talk too much about themselves and do not listen intently enough to women. The lady may feel unimportant and undervalued, appearing arrogant and self-absorbed. For instance, a male may discuss his recent promotion at work without inquiring about the woman's employment or hobbies, giving her the impression that she is not a significant part of the conversation.

Not observing nonverbal clues is another error. A lady may seem uncomfortable or not interested in the conversation if, for instance, she is crossing her arms or turning away.

Talking over or interrupting the woman is another error. This could give the impression that the woman's ideas and opinions are unimportant and be interpreted as rude and dismissive. For instance, it could be difficult for a woman to voice her ideas and opinions while a male is talking over her.

Not respecting personal boundaries is another typical error. Examples include approaching a lady with too many intimate inquiries or failing to honor her refusals. As a result, a woman may feel disrespected and uneasy, which could strain the bond between them. For instance, a male might inquire about a woman's past relationships on their first date, giving her the impression that she has no control over her limits.

Men should try to actively listen, pay attention to nonverbal clues, show interest in what the woman says, and respect her boundaries to avoid these typical communication blunders. To have a more seamless and productive conversation, men should also be conscious of their communication style and try to adjust to the women's.

In conclusion, developing solid and fulfilling relationships with women requires an awareness of and avoidance of the typical communication errors that males make. Men can enhance their communication abilities and forge closer bonds with women by being conscious of these errors and striving to rectify them.

9. How To Comprehend Boys

There are differences between the minds of boys and girls. Boys tend to be more visually focused. Compared to females, guys have more testosterone. Because of these innate differences, boys and girls approach life and problem-solving differently.

10. How To Navigate The Virtual World

Help your daughter come to terms with the fact that the online world is not the real one. Make sure she spends less time on her social media and more time with you and your family. She is more likely to get depressed about what other women have that she does not—their bodies, their outfits, or their partners—the more time she spends online. Set a rule prohibiting using a phone when eating, driving (absolutely!), and sleeping in her bedroom.

..11. How to Handle Illustrated Material

Because of their visual orientation, men are more inclined to use pornography, although girls can also fall victim to it. Thus, be truthful with her. Tell her that our bodies are programmed to be attracted to and excited by sexual stimuli, just like a boy would. But caution her that viewing porn will send her down a bad spiritual and emotional path.

Additionally, I stressed to her that the visuals found in pornography are often over the top and that she shouldn't take this as the gold standard for her sexuality. Tell her that she can refuse males and that she is under no obligation to consent to anything in the sexual area that makes her uncomfortable or that might be influenced by pornography when more boys show an interest in pornography.

12. How to Put in a Lot of Work

Assist your daughter in realizing that perseverance is the secret to success in life. Appreciate her efforts. Establish the link in her own life between her achievements and her diligence.

13 Ways To Be Faithful

A solid religious foundation will help your daughter deal with life's challenges. It will be the cornerstone upon which her judgment and standards will rest. Show her the importance of faith. Show her how to strengthen her faith. Join her in prayer.

14. Instruct her that bodies differ in terms of size and shape.

But instead of talking about your daughter's appearance and weight, focus on her health. She will be exposed to unrealistic and judgmental ideas about body image through the media. If you worry about her body or your own, your daughter will catch on and develop the same obsession. Rather, encourage and support her by complimenting her on things unrelated to her appearance.

15. Encourage her to try new things and be active.

But do not force or confine your daughter to any activity. The body is excellent for various tasks, including standing, thinking, laughing, playing sports, dancing, and learning. Encourage your daughter to be active because it makes her feel good or because she makes new friends rather than focusing on her weight.

16. Show her how to properly care for her entire body.

Encourage your daughter to eat three regular meals and two healthy snacks each day, along with five fruits and veggies, and limit her intake of sugary beverages. You should also exercise frequently, get adequate sleep, and adopt healthy eating habits. Safety and good personal hygiene are also crucial.

17. Show Her How the Body Functions

The body is beautiful; educating your daughter about the different—and typical—body parts and functions, like the bladder, pelvic area, and vagina, will make her feel more comfortable and secure in her flesh. You can be general and abstract at this age, but try to avoid confusion by using anatomically exact terminology.

18. Inform Her About Her Physical Changes During Puberty

Your goal is to prepare your kid for these changes in her body before they happen. In particular, understanding reproductive health and menstruation is critical for your daughter. Dr. Unger says that helping young girls understand the predictable changes their bodies are about to go through in a developmentally appropriate way might ease the road ahead. Knowing what to expect from her body changes will help your daughter feel less ashamed.

Ability to Correspond and Assent:

Strong communication and consent skills are essential in relationships. Sexual education gives women the tools to express their desires, limits, and concerns clearly and forcefully. It emphasizes complete focus, empathy, and respect for the partner's boundaries. Women can establish strong and mutually beneficial close relationships by promoting open communication.

Savagery with Personal Accomplices:

Sexual education addresses the problem of intimate partner violence (IPV), provides information about identifying signs of abuse and accessing services, and teaches women about the components of IPV, consent in intimate relationships, and safe exit strategies from oppressive environments. It also teaches women about healthy relationship components and fostering flexibility, which helps them protect their financial security and create relationships free from violence.

Decisions about Contraception and Nurturing:

Sexual education recognizes that women may become parents at different stages of their lives. It provides information on childrearing skills, development, and resources for expectant and new mothers. It also covers accessible reproductive options such as assisted reproductive technologies and birth control, enabling women to make decisions that are in line with their circumstances and goals.

Social and Restricted Thoughts:

Sexual education acknowledges and values the diversity of social and strict beliefs that surround sexuality. It provides a forum for discussing the intersections of social characteristics, cultural norms, and sexual health.

Admission for Sexual Health Services:

Sexual education emphasizes the importance of accessible medical providers, facilities, and resources where women can seek out sexual and reproductive health services, such as STI testing, contraception, and screenings for contraceptive-related medical issues. It also provides information on medical coverage options and rights to medical services, enabling women to make educated decisions about their healthcare needs.

In-depth Education:

Sexual education for women views sex education as an ingrained process. It emphasizes the need to stay up to date on emerging research on sexual health, advancements in regenerative medicine, and shifts in sexual norms and practices. Encouraging women to engage in ongoing education and introspection helps them discover their sexual well-being at different stages of life.

Peer Support and Local Community Engagement:

Sexual education encourages women to seek out support from their peers and participate in local drives focused on sexual health and prosperity. It also advances the creation of safe spaces where women can seek guidance, share experiences, and form stable organizations. Finally, local commitment helps women overcome.

Comprehensive sexual education is necessary.

This section revolves around the importance of comprehensive sexual education, with a focus on women's sexual health, pleasure, and consent. It includes the necessity of providing women with accurate and thorough information as well as engaging them with information about their bodies and sexual rights.

However, traditional approaches to sexual education have often been narrowly focused, focusing primarily on mental health and the prevention of physically transmitted infections. These approaches have disregarded important aspects of women's sexual prosperity, such as pleasure, co-sent, and body-grasping.

Full sexual education seeks to fill these gaps by providing a holistic and all-inclusive approach to women's sexual health. It views sexuality as a normal and characteristic aspect of human life and emphasizes the importance of promoting positive views, fostering healthy relationships, and providing accurate information.

A crucial component of comprehensive sexual education is the inclusion of information about women's sexual ecstasy. Ultimately, discussions regarding ecstasy have been minimized or disregarded, particularly about women's sexuality. Women who receive information and education on this topic can develop a better understanding of their bodies, desires, and impulses. This knowledge can increase sexual fulfillment, bravery, and overall well-being.

Section Four

What happens if they decline to ask?

Some kids may not ask many questions about relationships and sex, but that doesn't mean they aren't interested; they may have picked up on the subliminal message that it's not a good idea to ask inquiries about these topics.

When this happens, it's your responsibility to adjust. You have to communicate to your child that you are willing to talk to them about relationships, love, and sex.

We haven't talked about sex much, so you may try telling them straight out, "I know, but I want to change that." Therefore, don't hesitate to ask me any questions you may have about it.

You may also begin looking for opportunities to question people.

For example, your child's mother's acquaintance is expecting. Try asking, "Have you noticed that Daniel's mother's stomach is expanding?" since she is expecting a child shortly. Are you aware of how the baby got into her body?

Then, watch the conversation as it unfolds.

These are some issues that they may be worried about:

1. How are infants made?

It's important to be ready to answer honestly and gently, considering the child's age, maturity, and level of preparedness when they pose this question.

Put as simply as possible for a little or older child, babies come from mommy's tummy or from mommy's uterus.

As a mother, you should ideally foster your child's body confidence early on. When kids get older, and you teach them about their bodies and use the right language when talking about the changes that come with puberty, these kinds of questions become easier to respond to.

2. Is it possible for young individuals to become parents?

"Yes, teenagers can become pregnant if they have sex, are releasing eggs, and have their period.

When responding to this well-known query about sexual health, one crucial statement is helpful. Ready? Here it is... To transport sperm to the ovum, the penis penetrates the vagina. The penis must be firm or erect to release the sperm. The male then places his erect penis inside the woman's vagina while they are both lying quite near to one another (contrary to what many young children believe, the penis is not removed from the man's boy and is replaced after the deed is done!). To elaborate, you may say that after the sperm has reached the ovum, a baby starts to develop. The u-erus, a highly powerful bag of muscle situated above the vagina, is where the baby develops (not in the belly!). The uterus gradually enlarges to accommodate the developing baby until the time comes for delivery. The vagina, which can be up to 1 cm wide and is one of the openings between the woman's legs, is where the baby is delivered. t is significant to note that following delivery, the uterus and vagina return to their pre-pregnancy sizes.

It could be important to stress that "having sex" or "making love"—which includes having children—is an adult action that is done by two people who are incredibly in love with one another.

3. "Were you a virgin when you got married?" or "Do you sleep with your father?"

Whether or not you answer these types of personal questions depends largely on how comfortable you are. Some parents don't think it's necessary to disclose this information and can only explain that a person's past and present sexual experiences are private. Tell your child you would respect their privacy and promise not to ask them similar questions when they're older. If you want to be more honest, you could say something like, "No, I was t a virgin when I married your dad, but the world was much different back then..."

Deathly illnesses such as AIDS were unimportant. When asked about your recent personal life, you might respond, "Yes, your dad and I do have sex because we love each other so much." You may have to make some interpretations about the questions' meanings when you are asked them. Your child can be more interested in your advice on how morals and values should be formed than your personal life. That is to say, rather than asking if mom and dad ever had sex before being married, he or she might be more interested in finding out if it is generally acceptable to have sex before marriage.

4. "What are birth control methods?"

Try to be positive when you talk to your youngster about contraceptives.

Sexually transmitted infections and pregnancy can both be avoided in people using contraceptives. All teenagers need to learn about contraception so they may make informed decisions.

It might be challenging to talk to your child about contraception, but it's important to do so to protect their health and welfare.

There are numerous safe and effective birth control alternatives available to teenagers who are sexually active or who are considering getting married. They are free to choose the strategy that works best for them. These include:

1. Long-acting reversible contraceptives, or LARC methods,

including hormonal implants, IUDs, and other forms of birth control. Depending on the treatment, these medically implanted contraceptives can prevent pregnancy for up to three to ten years without the need for any additional follow-up care.

2. Quick hormonal methods

the s ot, the vaginal r ng, the patch, and the tablets—including the little pills—all of them. For these prescription treatments to be effective, patients must take them daily, weekly, monthly, or every three months (shot).

3. Barrier methods

Some examples are the cervical cap, sponge, diaphragm, and condoms. They have to be followed each time someone has sex. After the diaphragm is fitted and a prescription for a cervical cap is written, there is no need for a clinic appointment for these treatments.

It's also critical to stress that, despite their potential for gr at success, contraceptives are not always dependable. The only way to guarantee one won't become pregnant or have an STD is to abstain from sexual activity.

5. "Why do females get periods?"

Giving your child an explanation of menstruation or "having your period" can be done in the following way: Girls begin preparing for puberty at the age of 8 or 9. It achieves this by forming an interior waterbed with supple skin and a tiny quantity of blood. When there isn't a child within, the uterus changes the waterbed every month by leaking out the old one. The drips are mostly water, even if they look like blood. You have to put a pad (sanitary napkin) inside your pants to catch the leaks when you're menstruating. Tell your child that we are glad that women and girls have menstruation since it is a sign that their uteruses are healthy and able to bear fruit in the future.

At this point, it would be important to clarify that the bodies of men also undergo nocturnal discharges or wet dreams to prepare for adulthood. Put another way, male testicles begin to release practice sperm from the age of 8 or 9. A few extra sperm may occasionally leave a tiny wet stain on boys' bedding or pajamas during the night.

Let me stress once more how delighted we are for boys to have wet dreams since it indicates that their testicles are in good health and that they will be like fathers.

The Sexy Nature of Dirty Talk

There's more to the sensual appeal of obscene discourse than just the unimaginable factors that surround it. Because men and women are built differently, men like representations to fulfill their visual needs, whereas women like to imagine and dream. It's not particularly unusual, erratic, or lopsided. Everyone has "dirty" thoughts, and just as Mel Gibson's character learns in "What Women Need," there's more activity going on in our brains during sex that goes unspoken.

The most important thing to understand is that talking nasty isn't dirty. There's nothing vile or inappropriate about it, and once that's understood, it doesn't take away the feeling of unthinkable, given the society we live in today, but rather improves it; there's a tendency toward "I'm expressing these things so anyone can hear, and it's alright," but there's also a tendency toward "I'm happy to the point that (emed name of individual here) can't hear me now; they wouldn't accept that these words are leaving my mouth." If you don't like the term "dirty talk," there are many other ways to phrase it, like an underhanded conversation.

It surprises me how hardwired people are. It's common for women to want to visualize, while men prefer to hear. Before anything is done, a man has to know what his spouse needs to do for them or what they need to do for them. Hearing the phrases yelled, moaned, whined, or whispered for most guys only makes them more bearable. Ladies prefer to hear words and visualize what those expressions or phrases mean to them, how their partner will react, or how something will feel, even if it's only a few seconds or milliseconds beforehand. This allows their minds to fully comprehend the possible possibilities, heightening their feelings.

Additionally, it creates a stronger sense of intimacy between the two people because, at that moment, you are sharing more than just your bodies—you are also sharing your thoughts, which results in a much deeper merging than would otherwise occur. Peaking nasty isn't just about telling the other person what they should or should not do; it's also about offering assistance and engaging in seductive yet pleasant redirection.

A previous example of redirection involved taking something that could be a laborious and potentially demeaning expression and turning it into something that helps to appease the other person's conscience. It aims to give the other person a sense of security and, as a result, makes them feel more confident and sexy. This ensures that the person is less trapped in their thoughts and more present when experiencing what is happening, as opposed to worrying, fussing, or simply not being as into it as possible.

Sex is amazing, incredible, and livable, and mind-blowing. There is no reason why two people shouldn't be able to communicate openly and honestly about exactly what they need, how they need it when they need it, and while still feeling sexy, confident, and most importantly, perfect by their partner, even if it's just between them.

DIRECTIONS TO START, STEP BY STEP

Whether rearranging the furniture, discussing that progress with your management, or having an affair with your partner, the hardest part of any change is always starting. A person needs three things to implement an improvement: the desire to affect change, the motivation to get things started, and the persistence to carry it out while paying little attention to the changes being made. It's okay if you don't feel comfortable taking the risk and trying one or two expressions. Even though our society exploits inferred rather than overt sexuality as a marketing tool, it is appropriate to be a little reserved. This is one of those themes where it is far easier to infer than to state things explicitly. Not everyone is comfortable diving right in, but there are ways to ease in gradually, go deeper each time, and push yourself a bit beyond.

Starting the conversation outside of the room is one way to get people to start talking nasty in the room. Though others won't be appropriate, many locations can work for this conversation. In the unlikely event that you would prefer to keep your questions to yourself, ask them about their feelings about the matter by bringing it up as you learned about something your friend did with their partner, mentioning that you were reading an article about it, or reading a novel that referred to it, and seeing what they thought of the t. The focus is currently being placed on dirty talk in a particular context rather than how you are learning about someone's feelings toward it. This depersonalization can let someone take the first step toward starting.

Another tactic is to try a few expressions on your partner in the middle of a sexual encounter and see how they react. In the unlikely event of a noticeable positive response, you can build on it and work at a more notable volume each time. If that seems too drastic right away, that's okay too. Another tactic would be to start incorporating it into your daily life through various forms of communication. Many other expressions provided at the end of this article can be used as "unique cases" or extremely commonplace remarks that don't necessarily need to start a conversation. Nevertheless, this method frequently results in more talking and conversation because of the simultaneous rush of finally saying something like this for everyone to hear and the subsequent rush of realizing how your partner reacts and wanting to see them react that way again.

One way to test things out is with an email written after a night of animalistic joy; start by telling your partner how much you enjoyed when they performed x, y, or z, and be interactive. Saying anything like "I appreciated when you put your thing in my thing" won't cut it today. It will likely cause more embarrassment than anything else. Use the names of your and their bodily parts that you learned in school, as well as slang phrases and elegant idioms, but don't be doubtful. Observe their response and proceed accordingly; although there is a slight possibility that they will not be receptive to receiving this kind of email, the likelihood of receiving a response in kind is considerable. This can also be done as a prelude to phone sex by filling in with the content.

Sexting, or dirty talk through text messaging, is referred to as the easiest way to start, along with email, because it allows the initiator to do so from in front of a screen or behind a console, giving the impression of secrecy, regardless of how well you know the recipient.

Talking to your partner over the phone about sex or sexual activities is another way to start a conversation about sex. The ideal place to do this is somewhere quiet and peaceful, where you feel extremely at ease with the surroundings and anyone else who might be there. For example, someone might be amicable when they realize their closest friend is in the room across from them, but they might not feel comfortable among their relatives in the next room. Comfort level is crucial, and as long as you are amiable, the written content, the words, and the demonstrations will get progressively more amiable with time.

Generally speaking, all that someone waits for is for the other person to say something first. The more often you do this, the more natural it will seem to you and the more comfortable I will be. Dirty talk should be lively, diverse, and sometimes very provocative, but perhaps most importantly, it should be endearing. The goal is to include something your partner and you can both fully enjoy, not anything that makes you uncomfortable.

www.ingramcontent.com/pod-product-compliance
Lightning Source LLC
Chambersburg PA
CBHW052134110526
44591CB00012B/1722